D1601322

BOSTON COMMON PRESS
Brookline, Massachusetts

1999

Copyright © 1999 by The Editors of *Cook's Illustrated*

Boston Common Press
17 Station Street
Brookline, Massachusetts 02445

ISBN 0-936184-34-5
Library of Congress Cataloging-in-Publication Data
The Editors of *Cook's Illustrated*
     How to cook garden vegetables: An illustrated step-by-step guide to preparing asparagus, broccoli, cabbage, cauliflower, eggplant, green beans, greens, peas, peppers, tomatoes, and zucchini./The Editors of *Cook's Illustrated*
1st ed.

     Includes 81 recipes and 19 illustrations
     ISBN 0-936184-34-5 (hardback): $14.95
     I. Cooking. I. Title
1999

Manufactured in the United States of America

Distributed by Boston Common Press, 17 Station Street, Brookline, MA 02445.

Cover and text design: Amy Klee
Recipe development: Bridget Lancaster and Anne Yamanaka
Series editor: Jack Bishop

HOW TO COOK GARDEN VEGETABLES

An illustrated step-by-step guide to
preparing asparagus, broccoli, cabbage,
cauliflower, eggplant, green beans, greens,
peas, peppers, tomatoes, and zucchini.

THE COOK'S ILLUSTRATED LIBRARY

Illustrations by John Burgoyne

CONTENTS

introduction

L ate every August, our family drives over to the local agricultural fair where the kids flock to the bumper cars, the flying school bus, the spinning tea cups, and the haunted double-wide trailer. For my part, I look forward to a quiet stroll in the 4-H tent to view the garden produce, including beets, onions, carrots, peppers, tomatoes, and sweet corn. There is much simple pleasure to be had from a summer garden, in the tilling of the soil, the planting of the seed, and then the nurturing of the young plant. As with cooking, gardening is not just about the end result but also about the process.

In my own garden, I grow many of the vegetables featured in this book—not because they are cheaper (each of my tomatoes probably costs at least $2 after the purchase of composted manure, weed barriers, and an automatic watering system) but because the flavor and texture is infinitely better than store-bought. The problem, of course, with vegetables, even those grown at home, is how to prepare them. Cauliflower can be a rather dull offering, and yet when stir-fried over high heat it takes on a rich, nutty flavor. Broccoli starts to break down after eight minutes of cooking, causing loss of color and that well-known odor. Peas are tricky— they are often mealy and dry. Although vegetable cookery seems simple, there is a lot to know.

As with all of our "how-to" books, each recipe is the result of extensive testing, many hours having been spent in the *Cook's* kitchen to find the best cooking method, the best pan, or the best combination of ingredients.

We have also published *How to Make a Pie, How to Make an American Layer Cake, How to Stir-Fry, How to Make Ice Cream, How to Make Pizza, How to Make Holiday Desserts, How to Make Pasta Sauces, How to Make Salad, How to Grill, How to Make Simple Fruit Desserts, How to Make Cookie Jar Favorites, How to Cook Holiday Roasts and Birds, How to Make Stew, How to Cook Shrimp and Other Shellfish,* and *How to Barbecue and Roast on the Grill.* Many other titles in this series will soon be available. To order other books, call us at (800) 611-0759. We are also the editors and publishers of *Cook's Illustrated,* a bimonthly publication about American home cooking. For a free trial copy of *Cook's,* call (800) 526-8442.

Christopher P. Kimball
Publisher and Editor
Cook's Illustrated

chapter one

VEGETABLE
BASICS

V EGETABLE COOKERY IS GENERALLY QUICK AND
easy. Even so, cooks are perplexed by vegetables. They wonder what is the best way to
cook a particular vegetable and are often in
desperate need of inspiration when it comes to choosing
simple flavorings. This book addresses both issues.

In the pages that follow, we examine the 13 most popu-
lar garden vegetables. We started by testing all the relevant
cooking methods and making some conclusions about
which methods are best for that particular vegetable. From
there, we offer master recipes that explain our preferred
techniques along with plenty of variations so that you can
produce vegetable side dishes that are interesting and varied.

8

As you will see, a number of cooking techniques are used repeatedly in this book. Here is an explanation of each method and its general pros and cons.

▦ BOILING

"Boiling" means cooking in an abundant amount of boiling water, at least enough to cover the vegetables by several inches. When referring to vegetables, the term "blanching" (which means cooking in boiling water until partially but not fully done) is often used. If the water is salted (use at least ½ teaspoon of salt per quart of water) during boiling or blanching, the vegetables will be nicely seasoned. Blanched vegetables are often sautéed to finish the cooking process; this is also when more seasonings can be added. Porous vegetables, such as cauliflower and broccoli, can become waterlogged and mushy when boiled.

▦ STEAMING

"Steaming" means cooking in a basket set over boiling water. It has similar effects as boiling, except that there is no possibility of seasoning vegetables with salt as they cook. Also, since the vegetables are above water as they steam, they absorb less liquid and don't become soggy.

▦ BRAISING

"Braising" refers to cooking in a covered pan with a small amount of liquid. Often a braise starts with sautéing the vegetables in some fat before adding the liquid. Steam from this liquid cooks the vegetable through and eventually becomes a sauce that seasons the vegetable.

▋▋ GRILLING

The intense heat of the grill caramelizes the exterior of vegetables and concentrates their flavors by driving off water. Vegetables should be brushed lightly with oil before grilling, and the grill surface should be meticulously scraped to prevent delicate vegetables from picking up off flavors. Vegetables should be grilled over a medium-hot fire—you should be able to hold your hand five inches above the cooking surface for four seconds.

▋▋ BROILING

"Broiling" is similar to grilling. The intense heat of the broiler browns the exterior of vegetables and causes water to be expelled and evaporated. Lightly oiled vegetables should be placed in a single layer on a rimmed baking sheet for broiling. Position the vegetables about four inches from the broiling element for the best results.

▋▋ SAUTÉING AND STIR-FRYING

Most vegetables can be cooked in a hot pan with a little oil or butter. Sautéing and stir-frying are similar, especially since we find that a skillet works well when stir-frying on an American stove. (A wok is designed to sit in a cylindrical fire pit and is ill-suited to a flat stove.) In general, stir-frying relies on oil, not butter, and uses very high temperatures. We find it best to stir-fry in a very large (12-inch) nonstick skillet so that the vegetables can be placed in a single layer and will cook as quickly as possible. Sautéing generally occurs at more moderate temperatures. You may use a regular or nonstick skillet here. Sautéing is appropriate for eggplant, tender greens, peppers, cherry tomatoes, and zucchini.

There are several other cooking methods that can be applied to vegetables that we have not considered in this book. We tested many vegetables in the microwave. Although this controversial kitchen tool did a decent job in some cases, it was never our favorite method. Often vegetables cooked unevenly and dried out in spots.

We understand the value of roasting many vegetables. However, for garden vegetables we find that we want to cook them faster. Grilling and broiling yield comparable results—the exterior caramelizes and flavors are concentrated—and these methods seem more appropriate to warm-weather cooking.

Finally, we recognize how delicious fried vegetables can be. However, most cooks are looking for simpler, lower-fat preparations that they can use on a daily basis. For this reason, we have not considered frying in this book.

chapter two

ASPARAGUS

ASPARAGUS PRESENTS ONLY ONE PREPARA-
tion issue—should the spears be peeled, or is
it better to discard the tough, fibrous ends
entirely? While peeled asparagus have a
silkier texture, we preferred the contrast between the peel
and inner flesh. Peeling is also a lot of work. We prefer to
simply snap off the tough ends and proceed with cooking
(*see* figure 1).

We investigated moist-heat cooking methods and found
that boiling and steaming yielded similar results. The delicate tips remained a bit crisper when the asparagus was
steamed, so that's our preferred method.

A second option for asparagus is stir-frying. The spears

must be cut into smaller pieces—about one-and-a-half inches is right. We found that there is no reason to precook asparagus before stir-frying. As long as you use a skillet large enough to hold the asparagus in a single layer, they will soften after about four minutes of stir-frying. Adding a fairly liquidy sauce (which will reduce quickly to a syrup) helps finish the cooking process.

A third option, and one that most cooks don't consider, is grilling or broiling. The intense dry heat concentrates the flavor of the asparagus, and the exterior caramelization makes the spears especially sweet. The result is asparagus with a heightened and—we think—delicious flavor.

Figure 1.

In our tests, we found that the tough, woody part of the stem will break off in just the right place if you hold the spear the right way. Hold the asparagus about halfway down the stalk; with the other hand, hold the cut end between the thumb and index finger about an inch or so up from the bottom; bend the stalk until it snaps.

♔

Master Recipe

Steamed Asparagus
serves four

➤ **NOTE:** *A large sauté pan or Dutch oven is the best pot for steaming asparagus. Steamed asparagus is rather bland, so we prefer to toss it with a flavorful vinaigrette.*

1½   **pounds asparagus, tough ends snapped off**
      (*see* **figure 1, page 13**)

▪▪ **INSTRUCTIONS:**

Fit wide saucepan with steamer basket. Add water, keeping water level below basket. Bring water to boil over high heat. Add asparagus to basket. Cover and steam until asparagus spears bend slightly when picked up and flesh at cut end yields when squeezed, 3 to 4 minutes for asparagus under ½ inch in diameter, 4 to 5 minutes for jumbo asparagus. Remove asparagus from basket and season as directed in variations.

⁞⁞ V A R I A T I O N S :

Steamed Asparagus with Lemon Vinaigrette

Combine 1½ tablespoons lemon juice, ½ teaspoon Dijon mustard, and ¼ teaspoon Tabasco sauce in small bowl. Whisk in 2 tablespoons extra-virgin olive oil and season with salt and pepper to taste. Follow Master Recipe, tossing steamed asparagus with dressing. Serve warm or at room temperature.

Steamed Asparagus with Ginger-Hoisin Vinaigrette

Combine 2½ tablespoons rice wine vinegar, 1½ tablespoons hoisin sauce, 2½ teaspoons soy sauce, and 1½ teaspoons minced fresh gingerroot in small bowl. Whisk in 1 ½ tablespoons canola oil and 1½ teaspoons Asian sesame oil. Follow Master Recipe, tossing steamed asparagus with dressing. Serve warm or at room temperature.

Master Recipe

Stir-Fried Asparagus
serves four

➤ **NOTE:** *Thick spears should be halved lengthwise and then cut into 1½-inch pieces to ensure that the center cooks through.*

½	cup chicken stock or low-sodium canned broth
½	teaspoon salt
¼	teaspoon ground black pepper
1 ½	tablespoons plus 1 teaspoon peanut oil
1 ½	pounds asparagus, tough ends snapped off
	(*see* figure 1, page 13) and cut on the bias into
	1½-inch pieces
3	medium garlic cloves, minced

▦ **INSTRUCTIONS:**

1. Combine stock, salt, and pepper in small bowl and set aside.

2. Heat 12-inch nonstick skillet over high heat until quite hot, 2 to 3 minutes. Add 1½ tablespoons oil and swirl to coat pan evenly (oil should shimmer in pan immediately.) Add asparagus in single layer and stir-fry, tossing every 45 seconds, until well browned, about 4 minutes.

3. Clear center of pan, add garlic, and drizzle with remaining 1 teaspoon oil. Mash garlic with back of spatula. Cook 10 seconds and mix garlic with asparagus. Add chicken broth mixture and cook until sauce is syrupy, about 30 seconds. Serve immediately.

VARIATIONS:

Thai-Style Stir-Fried Asparagus with Chiles, Garlic, and Basil

Follow Master Recipe, replacing stock, salt, and pepper with 2 tablespoons soy sauce, 1 tablespoon water, and 1 tablespoon sugar. Add 1 tablespoon minced jalapeño or serrano chile with garlic. Off heat, stir in ¼ cup chopped fresh basil leaves. Serve immediately.

Stir-Fried Asparagus with Black Bean Sauce

Follow Master Recipe, reducing chicken stock to 2 tablespoons, omitting salt, and adding 3 tablespoons dry sherry, 1 tablespoon soy sauce, 1 tablespoon Asian sesame oil, 1 tablespoon fermented black beans, and 1 teaspoon sugar to bowl in step 1. Add 1½ teaspoons minced fresh gingerroot with garlic. Off heat, stir in 2 thinly sliced scallions. Serve immediately.

♛

Master Recipe

Grilled or Broiled Asparagus
serves four

➤ **NOTE:** *Thick spears will burn on the surface before they cook through. Use spears no thicker than ⅝ inch.*

1½   pounds asparagus, tough ends snapped off
(*see* figure 1, page 13)

1   tablespoon extra-virgin olive oil
Salt and ground black pepper

⸬ **INSTRUCTIONS:**

1. Light grill or preheat broiler. Toss asparagus with oil in medium bowl or, if broiling, on rimmed baking sheet.

2. Grill asparagus over medium heat, turning once, until tender and streaked with light grill marks, 5 to 7 minutes, or line up spears in single layer on baking sheet and broil, placing pan about 4 inches from broiler and shaking it once halfway through cooking to rotate spears, until tender and browned in some spots, 5 to 7 minutes. Season asparagus with salt and pepper to taste and serve hot, warm, or at room temperature.

⸫ **VARIATIONS:**

Grilled or Broiled Asparagus with Peanut Sauce

Whisk 1 minced garlic clove, 1½ teaspoons minced fresh gingerroot, 1½ teaspoons rice wine vinegar, 1½ teaspoons soy sauce, 1 tablespoon Asian sesame oil, 1 tablespoon smooth peanut butter, 1 tablespoon water, and salt and pepper to taste together in small bowl. Follow Master Recipe, tossing asparagus with half of this mixture instead of olive oil. Cook as directed. Whisk 1 tablespoon minced fresh cilantro leaves into remaining dressing. Toss cooked asparagus with dressing and adjust seasonings.

Grilled or Broiled Asparagus with Rosemary and Goat Cheese

Whisk ½ teaspoon minced fresh rosemary, 1 minced garlic clove, 1 tablespoon lemon juice, 2 tablespoons extra-virgin olive oil, and salt and pepper to taste together in small bowl. Follow Master Recipe, tossing asparagus with 1 tablespoon of this mixture instead of olive oil. Cook as directed. Toss cooked asparagus with remaining dressing, adjust seasonings, and sprinkle with 1 ounce crumbled goat cheese.

chapter three

BROCCOLI

ROCCOLI REQUIRES A MOIST-HEAT COOKING method to keep the florets tender and to cook through the stalks. We tested boiling, blanching then sautéing, and steaming. Boiled broccoli is soggy tasting and mushy, even when cooked for just two minutes. The florets absorb too much water. We found the same thing happened when we blanched the broccoli for a minute and then finished cooking it in a hot skillet.

Delicate florets are best cooked above water in a steamer basket. The stalk may be cooked along with the florets as long as it has been peeled and cut into small chunks. (*See* figures 2 and 3 for preparation.) Broccoli will be fully cooked after about five minutes of steaming. At this point, it may be tossed with a flavorful dressing. A warning: Cook broccoli just two or three minutes too long and chemical changes cause loss of color and texture.

We tried stir-frying broccoli without precooking and found that the florets started to fall apart long before the stems were tender. While blanching and then stir-frying helped the broccoli to cook more evenly, the florets were soggy. We found that partially cooking the broccoli in the steamer basket and then adding it to the stir-fry pan works best. Try this technique when you want to sauce broccoli rather than dress it with vinaigrette.

Figure 2.
Place head of broccoli upside down on a cutting board and trim off the florets very close to their heads with a large knife.

Figure 3.
The stalks may also be cooked. Stand each stalk up on the cutting board and remove the outer ⅛-inch from each side. Now cut the stalk in half lengthwise and into bite-sized pieces.

Master Recipe

Steamed Broccoli
serves four

➤ **N O T E** : *For maximum absorption, toss steamed broccoli with the dressings listed in the variations when hot. The broccoli may be served immediately or cooled to room temperature.*

1½   pounds broccoli (about 1 medium bunch),
       prepared according to figures 2 and 3 (page 21)

I N S T R U C T I O N S :

Fit wide saucepan with steamer basket. Add water, keeping water level below basket. Bring water to boil over high heat. Add broccoli to basket. Cover and steam until broccoli is just tender, 4½ to 5 minutes. Remove broccoli from basket and season as directed in variations.

V A R I A T I O N S :

Steamed Broccoli with Spicy Balsamic Dressing and Black Olives

Whisk 2 teaspoons balsamic vinegar, 2 teaspoons red wine vinegar, 1 minced garlic clove, ½ teaspoon hot red pepper flakes, and ¼ teaspoon salt in small bowl. Whisk in ¼ cup extra-virgin olive oil. Follow Master Recipe, tossing steamed broccoli with dressing and 12 large pitted and quartered black olives.

Steamed Broccoli with Orange-Ginger Dressing and Walnuts

In food processor combine 1 tablespoon peanut oil, 1 tablespoon soy sauce, 1 tablespoon honey, 1 tablespoon grated orange zest, 3 tablespoons orange juice, 1 peeled garlic clove, 1-inch piece peeled fresh gingerroot, and ½ teaspoon salt and process until smooth. Follow Master Recipe, tossing steamed broccoli with dressing, 2 thinly sliced scallions, and ⅔ cup toasted and chopped walnuts.

Steamed Broccoli with Lime-Cumin Dressing

Whisk 1 teaspoon grated lime zest, 1 tablespoon lime juice, ½ teaspoon ground cumin, ½ teaspoon salt, and hot red pepper sauce to taste in bowl. Whisk in 3 tablespoons extra-virgin olive oil, and then add ¼ cup minced red onion. Follow Master Recipe, tossing steamed broccoli with dressing.

Steamed Broccoli with Spanish Green Herb Sauce

In food processor, combine 2 peeled garlic cloves, ½ cup each tightly packed fresh cilantro and parsley leaves, 3 tablespoons extra-virgin olive oil, 1 tablespoon lemon juice, and ½ teaspoon salt and process until smooth. Follow Master Recipe, tossing steamed broccoli with dressing.

Master Recipe

Stir-Fried Broccoli
serves four

➤ **NOTE:** *Instead of steaming broccoli until tender and tossing it with a dressing, it may be partially steamed and then stir-fried with seasonings.*

½   cup chicken stock or canned low-sodium broth
½   teaspoon salt
      Ground black pepper
1½   tablespoons plus 1 teaspoon peanut oil
1   recipe Steamed Broccoli (page 22), cooked just 2½ minutes and removed from steamer
1   tablespoon minced garlic

INSTRUCTIONS:

1. Mix together chicken stock, salt, and pepper to taste in small bowl.

2. Heat 12-inch nonstick skillet over high heat until quite hot, 2 to 3 minutes. Add 1½ tablespoons oil and swirl to coat bottom of pan (oil should shimmer immediately). Add steamed broccoli and cook, stirring every 30 seconds, until fully cooked and heated through, about 2½ minutes.

3. Clear center of pan, add garlic, and drizzle with remaining 1 teaspoon oil. Mash garlic with back of spatula. Cook 10 seconds and then mix garlic with broccoli. Add chicken stock mixture and cook until sauce is syrupy, about 30 seconds. Serve immediately.

⁝ VARIATIONS:

Stir-Fried Broccoli with Orange Sauce

Follow Master Recipe, reducing chicken stock to 1½ tablespoons and combining with 3 tablespoons orange juice, 1½ teaspoons grated orange zest, ¼ teaspoon sugar, and 2 teaspoons soy sauce; omit salt. Reduce garlic to 1 clove and add 1 medium scallion, thinly sliced, and 1 teaspoon minced fresh gingerroot along with garlic.

Stir-Fried Broccoli with Hot-and-Sour Sauce

Follow Master Recipe, reducing chicken stock to 1 tablespoon and combining with 3 tablespoons cider vinegar, 1 tablespoon soy sauce, and 2 teaspoons sugar; omit salt. Substitute ginger for garlic and add 1 tablespoon minced jalapeño or other fresh chile along with ginger in step 3.

chapter four

CABBAGE
& BRUSSELS
SPROUTS

LARGE GREEN CABBAGE AND SMALL BRUSSELS sprouts have similar cooking properties. Both become waterlogged when boiled. Steaming leaves cabbage and Brussels sprouts less soggy, but the flavor is wan and listless. Cabbage and Brussels sprouts need a cooking method that will add some flavor as well as counter their strong mustardy smell.

We found that shredding cabbage (*see* figures 4 to 6) and braising it in a mixture of butter and chicken stock adds flavor. As long as the amount of liquid is quite small (a tablespoon was enough to cook a pound of cabbage), the texture will still be a bit crunchy and delicious. Cabbage can also be braised in other fats (bacon drippings) and liquids (apple juice, wine). Cream combines fat and liquid and may be used alone.

Brussels sprouts can easily be cooked by simmering them in water, draining, and then sautéing in seasonings. This method is awkward with shredded cabbage but works well with the small, round sprouts. We tested steaming the sprouts as well as braising them in a little salted water. The sprouts benefited greatly from cooking with some salt. As with cabbage, Brussels sprouts may also be braised in cream and served as is.

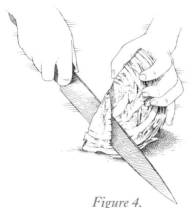

Figure 4.
Cut cabbage into quarters and use a chef's knife to remove the tough core section from each piece.

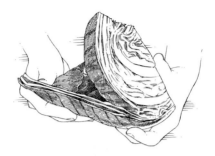

Figure 5.
Pull off several cabbage leaves at a time and press them flat
against a cutting board.

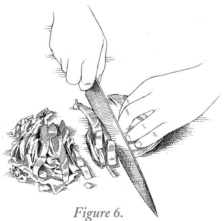

Figure 6.
Use a chef's knife to cut each stack of cabbage diagonally into
¼-inch-wide shreds.

28

♛

Master Recipe

Braised Cabbage
serves four

➤ NOTE: *This recipe uses about six cups of shredded cabbage.*

1	tablespoon unsalted butter
1	tablespoon chicken stock or low-sodium canned broth
½	large head green cabbage (about 1½ pounds), cored and cut into ¼-inch shreds (*see* figures 4 through 6)
¼	teaspoon dried thyme
1	tablespoon minced fresh parsley leaves
	Salt and ground black pepper

▦ INSTRUCTIONS:

Heat butter in large skillet over medium heat. Add stock, then cabbage and thyme. Bring to simmer; cover and continue to simmer, stirring occasionally, until cabbage is wilted but still bright green, 7 to 9 minutes. Sprinkle with parsley and season with salt and pepper to taste. Serve immediately.

█ VARIATIONS:

Cream-Braised Cabbage with Lemon and Shallots
Follow Master Recipe, replacing butter and chicken stock with ¼ cup heavy cream, 1 teaspoon lemon juice, and 1 small minced shallot. Omit thyme and parsley.

Braised Cabbage with Bacon and Onion
Fry 4 strips bacon in large skillet over medium heat until crisp, about 5 minutes. Remove bacon from pan with slotted spoon and drain on paper towels. Pour off all but 1 table-spoon bacon drippings. Add ½ small onion, minced, to drippings, and sauté until slightly colored, 1½ minutes. Proceed with Master Recipe, omitting butter. Crumble bacon over cooked cabbage and serve.

Braised Cabbage with Caraway and Mustard
Follow Master Recipe, replacing stock with 1 tablespoon apple juice and ½ teaspoon Dijon mustard and substituting 1 tablespoon caraway seeds for parsley.

Master Recipe

Braised Brussels Sprouts
serves three to four

➤ **NOTE:** *After cooking you may toss Brussels sprouts with a little butter and season them with ground black pepper. Or try one of the variations that follow. In our testing, we found no benefit to cutting an X into the bottom of each sprout. (Some sources say this promotes even cooking.) Simply trim the bottom of the stem and remove any discolored leaves before cooking.*

1   **pound small Brussels sprouts, stems trimmed and any discolored outer leaves removed**
½   **teaspoon salt**

⠿ INSTRUCTIONS:

Bring sprouts, ½ cup water, and salt to boil in large skillet over heat. Lower heat to medium, cover, and simmer (shaking pan once or twice to redistribute sprouts) until knife tip inserted into center of sprout meets little resistance, 8 to 10 minutes. Drain well and season as directed in variations or note above.

▐▐ **VARIATIONS:**

Brussels Sprouts Braised in Cream

Follow Master Recipe, substituting 1 cup heavy cream for water. Increase cooking time to 10 to 12 minutes. Season with pinch grated nutmeg and ground black pepper and serve without draining.

Glazed Brussels Sprouts with Chestnuts

If chestnuts are unavailable, substitute ⅓ cup toasted, chopped hazelnuts.

Prepare Master Recipe and set drained Brussels sprouts aside. Heat 2 tablespoons unsalted butter and 1 tablespoon sugar in large skillet over medium-high heat until butter melts and sugar dissolves. Stir in 16-ounce can peeled chestnuts in water, drained. Turn heat to low and cook, stirring occasionally, until chestnuts are glazed, about 3 minutes. Add 1 tablespoon unsalted butter and cooked Brussels sprouts. Cook, stirring occasionally, until heated through, 3 to 4 minutes. Season with salt and pepper to taste and serve immediately.

Brussels Sprouts with Garlic and Pine Nuts

Prepare Master Recipe and set drained Brussels sprouts aside. Heat 2 tablespoons extra-virgin olive oil in large skillet over medium heat. Add ¼ cup pine nuts and cook, stirring occasionally, until nuts begin to brown, about 2

3 2

minutes. Add 2 minced garlic cloves and cook until soft-ened, about 1 minute. Stir in cooked Brussels sprouts. Cook, stirring occasionally, until heated through, 3 to 4 minutes. Season with salt and pepper to taste and serve immediately.

Brussels Sprouts with Tarragon-Mustard Butter

The mustard sauce may separate and appear curdled after the sprouts are added. If so, continue cooking and it should come back together.

Prepare Master Recipe and set drained Brussels sprouts aside. Melt 4 tablespoon unsalted butter in large skillet over medium heat. Whisk in 2 tablespoons Dijon mustard until smooth. Add 1 teaspoon dried tarragon leaves. Cook, stir-ring constantly, until bubbly, about 30 seconds. Stir in sprouts, coating well with sauce. Cook, stirring frequently, until heated through, 3 to 4 minutes. Season to taste with salt and pepper and serve immediately.

chapter five

CAULIFLOWER

AULIFLOWER IS VERY POROUS, WHICH CAN BE an advantage or a disadvantage depending on the cooking technique used. We found that boiled cauliflower, even when underdone, always tastes watery. Steaming is much better, producing a clean, bright, sweet flavor and a crisp-tender, not soggy, texture.

To confirm our sensory observations, we weighed cauliflower before and after cooking and noticed a 10 percent increase in weight when the cauliflower was boiled (the extra weight was all water) and no change in weight when the cauliflower was steamed. After steaming, cauliflower may be dressed with a vinaigrette or sautéed briefly in a flavorful fat.

A second option is braising, which takes advantage of cauliflower's ability to absorb liquid. We found that it is best to sauté the cauliflower first—browning intensifies the naturally mild flavor of cauliflower and adds a layer of sweetness—then add a flavorful liquid. Browned cauliflower takes well to aggressive seasonings, such as soy sauce, Indian spices, or even chiles.

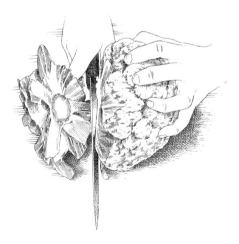

Figure 7.
To prepare cauliflower, start by pulling off the outer leaves and trimming off the stem near the base of the head.

Figure 8.
Turn the cauliflower upside down so the stem is facing up.
Using a sharp knife, cut around the core to remove it.

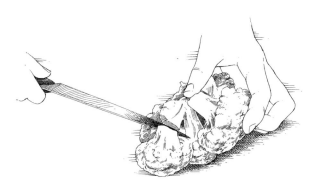

Figure 9.
Separate the individual florets from the inner stem using the tip
of a chef's knife.

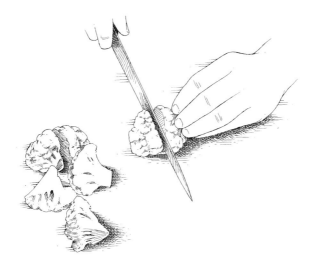

Figure 10.
Cut the florets in half, or in quarters if necessary, so that indi-
vidual pieces are about 1 inch square.

♛

Master Recipe

Steamed Cauliflower
serves four

➤ **NOTE:** *Mild seasonings, such as dill, basil, nuts, and citrus, are the best complement to the fresh, delicate flavor of steamed cauliflower. You may toss steamed cauliflower with extra-virgin olive oil or butter and salt and serve as is, or follow any of the simple variations.*

1   medium head cauliflower (about 2 pounds),
trimmed, cored, and cut into florets
(*see* figures 7 through 10, pages 35 to 37)

▩ **INSTRUCTIONS:**

Fit wide saucepan with steamer basket. Fill with enough water to reach just below bottom of basket. Bring water to boil over high heat. Add cauliflower to basket. Cover and steam until cauliflower is tender but still offers some resistance to the tooth when sampled, 7 to 8 minutes. Remove cauliflower from basket and season as directed in variations or note above.

▩ **VARIATIONS:**

Steamed Cauliflower with Dill-Walnut Vinaigrette
Whisk 1 teaspoon Dijon mustard, 1 tablespoon red wine vinegar, 1 tablespoon lemon juice, ½ minced shallot or scal-

lion, 2 tablespoons minced fresh dill, 2 tablespoons extra-virgin olive oil, and salt and pepper to taste in small bowl. Follow Master Recipe, tossing steamed cauliflower with dressing and ½ cup toasted, chopped walnuts. Serve warm or at room temperature.

Steamed Cauliflower with Curry-Basil Vinaigrette

Whisk 1 tablespoon lemon juice, 1 tablespoon white wine vinegar, 1 teaspoon curry powder, 1½ teaspoons honey, ¼ teaspoon salt, and ⅛ teaspoon pepper together in small bowl. Whisk in 3 tablespoons extra-virgin olive oil and then add 2 tablespoons chopped fresh basil leaves. Follow Master Recipe, tossing steamed cauliflower with dressing. Serve warm or at room temperature.

Steamed Cauliflower with Bread Crumbs, Capers, and Chopped Egg

Follow Master Recipe, setting steamed cauliflower aside. Heat 2 tablespoons butter in large skillet over medium heat until foamy. Add 3 tablespoons dried plain bread crumbs and cook, stirring occasionally, until lightly browned, about 5 minutes. Add cauliflower and heat through, about 1 minute. Add 1½ tablespoons lemon juice, 2 tablespoons minced fresh parsley leaves, 2 tablespoons drained capers, and 1 hard-boiled egg, pressed through a sieve to crumble very fine. Toss lightly, season with salt and pepper to taste, and serve immediately.

Browned and Braised Cauliflower with Asian Flavors

serves four

➤ **NOTE:** *The stronger flavor of browned cauliflower stands up well to bolder, more complex flavor combinations, such as the garlic, ginger, sesame oil, and soy sauce used in this recipe.*

2	tablespoons soy sauce
2	tablespoons rice wine vinegar
1	tablespoon dry sherry
1½	tablespoons canola oil
1	medium head cauliflower, trimmed, cored, and cut into florets (*see* figures 7 through 10, pages 35 to 37)
2	medium garlic cloves, minced
2	tablespoons minced fresh gingerroot
1	teaspoon Asian sesame oil
2	medium scallions, white and green parts, minced
	Ground black pepper

▦ **INSTRUCTIONS:**

1. Combine soy sauce, vinegar, sherry, and ¼ cup water in small bowl and set aside.

2. Heat large skillet over medium-high heat until pan is very hot, 3 to 4 minutes. Add canola oil, swirling pan to coat evenly. Add florets and sauté, stirring occasionally, until they begin to brown, 6 to 7 minutes.

3. Clear center of pan, add garlic and ginger, and drizzle with sesame oil. Mash garlic-ginger mixture with back of spatula and cook until fragrant, about 1 minute. Stir to combine garlic-ginger mixture with cauliflower. Sauté for 30 seconds.

4. Reduce heat to low and add soy sauce mixture. Cover and cook until florets are fully tender but still offer some resistance to the tooth when sampled, 4 to 5 minutes. Add scallions and toss lightly to distribute. Season with pepper to taste and serve immediately.

Browned and Braised Cauliflower
with Indian Flavors
serves four

➤ **NOTE:** *Yogurt creates a rich and satisfying sauce that tames and blends the flavors of the spices. If you like, add ½ cup thawed frozen green peas along with the cilantro.*

¼	cup plain yogurt
1	tablespoon lime juice
1½	tablespoons canola oil
1	medium head cauliflower, trimmed, cored, and cut into florets (*see* figures 7 through 10, pages 35 to 37)
½	medium onion, sliced thin
1	teaspoon ground cumin
1	teaspoon ground coriander
1	teaspoon ground turmeric
¼	teaspoon hot red pepper flakes
¼	cup chopped fresh cilantro leaves
	Salt and ground black pepper

▓ **INSTRUCTIONS:**

1. Combine yogurt, lime juice, and ¼ cup water in small bowl and set aside.

2. Heat large skillet over medium-high heat until pan is

42

very hot, 3 to 4 minutes. Add oil, swirling pan to coat evenly. Add florets and sauté, stirring occasionally, until they begin to soften, 2 to 3 minutes. Add onions; continue sautéing until florets begin to brown and onions soften, about 4 minutes.

3. Stir in cumin, coriander, turmeric, and pepper flakes; sauté until spices begin to toast and are fragrant, 1 to 2 minutes. Reduce heat to low and add yogurt mixture. Cover and cook until flavors meld, about 4 minutes. Add cilantro, toss to distribute, cover, and cook until florets are fully tender but still offer some resistance to the tooth when sampled, about 2 minutes more. Season with salt and pepper to taste and serve immediately.

chapter six

EGGPLANT

HE BIGGEST CHALLENGE THAT CONFRONTS the cook when preparing eggplant is excess moisture. While the grill will evaporate this liquid and allow the eggplant to brown nicely, this won't happen under the broiler or in a hot pan. The eggplant will steam in its own juices. The result is an insipid flavor and mushy texture.

Salting is the classic technique for drawing some moisture out of the eggplant before cooking. We experimented with both regular table salt and kosher salt and prefer kosher salt because the crystals are large enough to wipe away after the salt has done its job. Finer table salt crystals dissolve into the eggplant flesh and must be flushed out with water. The eggplant must then be thoroughly dried, which adds more prep time, especially if the eggplant has been diced for sautéing. (We prefer to dice eggplant that will be sautéed to increase the surface area that can brown and absorb flavorings.)

Eggplant destined for the broiler should be sliced very thin (about ¼ inch thick) so that the salt can work quickly. The salt will take more time to penetrate thicker slices and will in the end be less effective. However, when grilling, you want thicker slices that won't fall apart on the cooking grate. We found that ¾-inch rounds are perfect for grilling.

♛

Master Recipe

Sautéed Eggplant
serves four

➤ **NOTE:** *Very small eggplants (under 6 ounces each) may be cooked without salting. However, we found that large eggplants generally have a lot of moisture, which is best removed before cooking.*

1	large eggplant (about 1½ pounds), ends trimmed and cut into ¾-inch cubes
1	tablespoon kosher salt
2	tablespoons extra-virgin olive oil
	Ground black pepper
1	medium garlic clove, minced
2-4	tablespoons minced fresh parsley or finely shredded basil leaves

⠿ **INSTRUCTIONS:**

1. Place eggplant in large colander and sprinkle with salt, tossing to coat evenly. Let stand 30 minutes. Using paper towels or large kitchen towel, wipe salt off and pat excess moisture from eggplant.

2. Heat oil in heavy-bottomed 12-inch skillet until it shimmers and becomes fragrant over medium-high heat. Add eggplant cubes and sauté until they begin to brown, about 4 minutes. Reduce heat to medium-low and cook, stirring occasionally, until eggplant is fully tender and lightly browned, 10 to 15 minutes. Stir in pepper to taste, and add garlic. Cook to blend flavors, about 2 minutes. Off heat, stir in herb, adjust seasonings, and serve immediately.

⁞ VARIATIONS:

Sautéed Eggplant with Crisped Bread Crumbs

Melt 2 tablespoons unsalted butter in small skillet. Add ½ cup plain dried bread crumbs and toast over medium-high heat until deep golden and crisp, stirring frequently, about 5 to 6 minutes. Follow Master Recipe, adding toasted bread crumbs with herb.

Sautéed Eggplant with Asian Garlic Sauce

Follow Master Recipe, substituting 2 tablespoons peanut or vegetable oil for olive oil and adding 2 teaspoons minced fresh gingerroot with garlic. Once garlic and ginger are in pan, cook to blend flavors, about 1 minute. Add mixture of 2 tablespoons soy sauce, 2 tablespoons rice wine vinegar, and 1 teaspoon sugar. Simmer until eggplant absorbs liquid, about 1 minute. Substitute 2 tablespoons minced fresh cilantro leaves and 2 tablespoons thinly sliced scallions for parsley or basil.

♛

Master Recipe

Broiled Eggplant
serves four

➤ NOTE: *For broiling, it's best to slice the eggplant very thin.*

1	large eggplant (about 1½ pounds), ends trimmed and sliced crosswise into ¼-inch-thick rounds
1	tablespoon kosher salt
3	tablespoons extra-virgin olive oil
2–3	tablespoons minced fresh parsley or finely shredded basil leaves
	Ground black pepper

▦ INSTRUCTIONS:

1. Place eggplant in large colander and sprinkle with salt, tossing to coat evenly. Let stand 30 minutes. Using paper towels or large kitchen towel, wipe salt off and pat excess moisture from eggplant.

2. Preheat broiler. Arrange eggplant slices on foil-lined baking sheet. Brush both sides with oil. Broil eggplant slices 4 inches from heat source until tops are mahogany brown, 3

48

to 4 minutes. Turn slices over and broil until other side browns, another 3 to 4 minutes.

3. Remove eggplant from oven and sprinkle with herb. Season with pepper to taste and serve hot, warm, or at room temperature.

■■ VARIATION:

Broiled Eggplant with Parmesan Cheese

This variation is delicious on its own or perfect as vegetarian main course for two when served with a basic tomato sauce.

Follow Master Recipe through step 2. Sprinkle cooked eggplant with ½ cup grated Parmesan cheese. Return eggplant to broiler until cheese melts and becomes bubbly and browned, 2 to 3 minutes. Sprinkle with parsley or basil and serve immediately.

👑

Master Recipe

Grilled Eggplant
serves four

➤ **NOTE:** *There's no need to salt eggplant destined for the grill. The intense grill heat will vaporize excess moisture. You may use oregano in place of thyme if desired.*

- 3 tablespoons extra-virgin olive oil
- 2 medium garlic cloves, minced
- 2 teaspoons minced fresh thyme or oregano leaves
- Salt and ground black pepper
- 1 large eggplant (about 1½ pounds), ends trimmed and cut crosswise into ¾-inch rounds

░ INSTRUCTIONS:

1. Light grill. Combine oil, garlic, herbs, and salt and pepper to taste in small bowl. Place eggplant on platter and brush both sides with oil mixture.

2. Grill eggplant, turning once, until both sides are marked with dark stripes, 8 to 10 minutes. Serve hot, warm, or at room temperature.

⁞⁞ VARIATION:

Grilled Eggplant with Ginger and Soy

Combine 2 tablespoons soy sauce, 1½ tablespoons honey, 1 tablespoon rice wine vinegar, and 1 tablespoon water in small skillet. Bring to boil over medium-high heat and simmer until slightly thickened, about 2 minutes. Remove from heat and add 1 teaspoon Asian sesame oil. Follow Master Recipe, substituting peanut oil for olive oil, using ginger in place of garlic, and omitting herb, salt and pepper. Drizzle thickened soy mixture over grilled eggplant, sprinkle with 2 thinly sliced scallions, and serve.

chapter seven

GREEN BEANS

E'VE FOUND THAT GREEN BEANS respond better to boiling than steaming. A pound of beans in a standard steamer basket will not cook evenly—the beans close to the steaming water cook more quickly than the beans at the top of the pile. Stirring the beans once or twice as they cook solves this problem, but it is somewhat dangerous to stick your hand into the hot pot. Boiling is simpler—just add the beans and cook until tender—and it permits the addition of salt during cooking.

Unlike other vegetables that can become soggy when

boiled, the thick skin on green beans keeps the texture crisp and firm. Leave beans whole when boiling; cut beans will become waterlogged. Boiled beans can be flavored with some butter or oil, dressed with a vinaigrette, or sautéed briefly in a flavorful fat.

A second cooking option is braising. We found that the thick skin on most beans means that they are fairly slow to absorb flavorful liquids like tomatoes, cream, or stock. For this reason, we had the best success when we braised the beans for a full 20 minutes.

Braised beans lose their bright green color. Older, tougher beans benefit from long cooking, but really fresh green beans are best boiled and then seasoned, so as to retain as much of their flavor and texture as possible.

Master Recipe

Boiled Green Beans
serves four

➤ **N O T E :** *The freshness and thickness of the beans can greatly affect cooking time. Thin, farm-fresh beans—not much thicker than a strand of cooked linguine—may be done in just 2 minutes. Most supermarket beans are considerably thicker and have traveled some distance, hence the 5-minute cooking time recommended below. Dress the beans with a drizzle of extra-virgin olive oil or a pat of butter as well as a generous sprinkling of salt and pepper. Or make one of the variations.*

1   pound green beans, ends snapped off
1   teaspoon salt

I N S T R U C T I O N S :

Bring 2½ quarts of water to boil in large saucepan. Add beans and salt and cook until tender, about 5 minutes. Drain and season as directed in variations or note above.

V A R I A T I O N S :

Green Beans with Toasted Walnuts and Tarragon
Other nuts, especially pine nuts and hazelnuts, and other herbs, especially parsley and basil, may be used in a similar fashion.

Follow Master Recipe, placing drained beans in large serving bowl. Add ¼ cup chopped and toasted walnuts and 1½ tablespoons minced fresh tarragon leaves. Drizzle with 1½ tablespoons walnut or extra-virgin olive oil and toss gently to coat. Sprinkle with salt and pepper to taste and serve warm or at room temperature.

Green Beans with Fresh Tomato, Basil, and Goat Cheese

Follow Master Recipe, placing drained beans in large serving bowl. Add ½ cup chopped fresh tomato, 2 tablespoons chopped fresh basil leaves, and 1 ounce crumbled goat cheese. Drizzle with 2 tablespoons extra-virgin olive oil and 1 teaspoon balsamic vinegar and toss gently to coat. Season with salt and pepper to taste and serve warm or at room temperature.

Green Beans with Bacon and Onion

Fry 4 strips bacon, cut into ½-inch pieces, in large skillet over medium heat until crisp, about 5 minutes. Remove bacon from pan with slotted spoon and drain on paper towels. Pour off all but 2 tablespoons bacon drippings. Add 1 medium onion, minced, to drippings and sauté until softened, about 5 minutes. Follow Master Recipe, adding drained beans to skillet. Toss to heat through, 1 to 2 minutes. Add bacon and season with salt (sparingly) and pepper to taste. Serve immediately.

Braised Green Beans, Italian Style
serves four

➤ **NOTE:** *The beans lose their bright green color but gain flavor from cooking in a tomato sauce.*

2   tablespoons extra-virgin olive oil
1   small onion, diced
2   medium garlic cloves, minced
1   cup chopped canned tomatoes
1   pound green beans, ends snapped off
    Salt and ground black pepper
2   tablespoons minced fresh parsley leaves

∷ INSTRUCTIONS:

1. Heat oil in large sauté pan over medium heat. Add onion and cook until softened, about 5 minutes. Add garlic and cook for 1 minute. Add tomatoes and simmer until juices thicken slightly, about 5 minutes.

2. Add green beans, ¼ teaspoon salt, and a few grindings of pepper to pan. Stir well, cover, and cook, stirring occasionally, until beans are tender but still have some bite, about 20 minutes. Stir in parsley and adjust seasonings. Serve immediately.

Braised Green Beans, Asian Style
serves four

➤ NOTE: *The braising liquid—chicken stock, soy sauce, and rice wine vinegar—cooks down to a concentrated, very flavorful sauce, which is especially delicious over rice.*

2	tablespoons peanut oil
4	medium scallions, sliced thin
2	medium garlic cloves, minced
¾	cup chicken stock or low-sodium canned broth
3	tablespoons soy sauce
1	tablespoon rice wine vinegar
2	teaspoons sugar
1	pound green beans, ends snapped off
	Ground black pepper
2	tablespoons minced fresh basil leaves

■ INSTRUCTIONS:

1. Heat oil in large sauté pan over medium heat. Add scallions and cook until softened, 2 to 3 minutes. Add garlic and cook for 1 minute. Add stock, soy sauce, vinegar, and sugar, and simmer until liquid thickens slightly, about 5 minutes.

2. Add green beans and a few grindings of pepper to pan. Stir well, cover, and cook, stirring occasionally, until beans are tender but still have some bite, about 20 minutes. Stir in basil and adjust seasonings. Serve immediately.

chapter eight

GREENS

MANY COOKS THINK THEY CAN TREAT ALL leafy greens the same way, even though some are delicate enough for salads while others seem as tough as shoe leather. After cleaning, stemming, and cooking more than a hundred pounds of leafy greens, we found that they fell into two categories, each of which is handled quite differently.

Spinach, beet greens, and Swiss chard are tender and rich in moisture. They require no additional liquid during cooking. They taste of the earth and minerals but are rather delicate. Kale as well as mustard, turnip, and collard greens are tougher and require the addition of some liquid as they cook. Their flavor is very assertive, even peppery in cases, and can be overwhelming.

We tested boiling, steaming, and sautéing tender greens. Boiling produced the most brilliantly colored greens, but they were also very mushy and bland. The water cooked out all their flavor and texture. Steamed greens were less mushy, but clearly these tender greens did not need any liquid. Damp greens that were tossed in a hot oil (which could be flavored with aromatics and spices) wilted in just two or three minutes in a covered pan. Once wilted, we found it best to remove the lid so the liquid in pan would evaporate. This method has the advantage of flavoring the greens as they cook.

Tougher greens don't have enough moisture to be wilted in a hot pan; they scorch before they wilt. Steaming these greens produces a better texture but does nothing to tame their bitter flavor. Tough greens benefit from cooking in some water, which will wash away some of their harsh notes.

We tested boiling two pounds of greens in an abundant quantity of salted water and what might be called shallow-blanching in just two quarts of salted water. We found that cooking the greens in lots of water diluted their flavor too much. Shallow blanching removes enough bitterness to make these assertive greens palatable, but not so much as to rob them of their character. Blanched greens should be drained and then briefly cooked with seasonings.

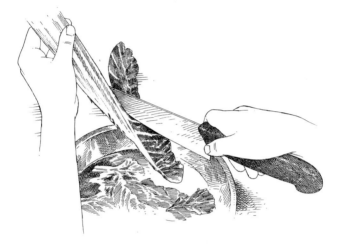

Figure 11.
To prepare Swiss chard, kale, collards, and mustard greens, hold
each leaf at the base of the stem over a bowl filled with water
and use a sharp knife to slash the leafy portion from either side of
the thick stem. Discard the stem.

Figure 12.
Turnip greens are most easily stemmed by grasping the leaf
between your thumb and index finger at the base of the stem and
stripping it off by hand.

Figure 13.
When using the above method with turnip greens, the very tip of
the stem will break off along with the leaves. It is tender enough
to cook along with the leaves.

61

♛

Master Recipe

Sautéed Tender Greens

serves four

➤ **NOTE:** *To stem spinach and beet greens, simply pinch off the leaves where they meet the stems. A thick stalks runs through each Swiss chard leaf, so it must be handled differently; see figure 11 on page 60 for information on this technique. A large, deep Dutch oven or even a soup kettle is best for this recipe.*

3   tablespoons extra-virgin olive oil
2   medium garlic cloves, minced
2   pounds damp tender greens, such as spinach, beet greens, or Swiss chard, stemmed, washed in several changes of cold water, and coarsely chopped
    Salt and ground black pepper
    Lemon wedges (optional)

▟ **INSTRUCTIONS:**

Heat oil and garlic in Dutch oven or other deep pot and cook until garlic sizzles and turns golden, about 1 minute. Add wet greens, cover, and cook over medium-high heat, stirring occasionally, until greens completely wilt, about 2 to 3 minutes. Uncover and season with salt and pepper to taste. Cook over high heat until liquid evaporates, 2 to 3 minutes. Serve immediately, with lemon wedges if desired.

▓ **VARIATIONS:**

Sautéed Tender Greens with Indian Spices

Follow Master Recipe, making these changes: Replace olive oil with 2 tablespoons vegetable oil. Cook 1 minced onion with garlic and oil. When onion and garlic are golden, add 1 teaspoon minced fresh gingerroot, ½ minced jalapeño chile, 2 teaspoons curry powder, and ½ teaspoon ground cumin. Cook until fragrant, about 2 minutes. Add wet greens and proceed with recipe. When liquid evaporates in pan, add ¼ cup heavy cream and 2 teaspoons brown sugar. Cook, uncovered, until cream thickens, about 2 minutes. Serve immediately.

Sautéed Tender Greens with Cumin, Tomato, and Cilantro

Follow Master Recipe, making these changes: Cook 1 minced onion with garlic and oil. When onion and garlic are golden, add ½ minced jalapeño chile and 1½ teaspoons ground cumin. Cook until fragrant, about 2 minutes. Add 2 large plum tomatoes, seeded and chopped, and cook until their juices release, about 1 minute. Add wet greens and proceed with recipe. When greens are done, add 2 tablespoons minced fresh cilantro leaves. Serve immediately, with lime wedges if desired.

Sautéed Tender Greens with Asian Flavors

Follow Master Recipe, making these changes: Replace olive oil with 2 tablespoons vegetable or peanut oil. Cook ½ teaspoon hot red pepper flakes with garlic. Add wet greens and proceed with recipe. When liquid in pan evaporates, add mixture of 1½ tablespoons soy sauce, 1 tablespoon Asian sesame oil, 2 teaspoons rice wine vinegar, and 2 teaspoons sugar. Cook until liquid almost evaporates, about 1 minute. Serve immediately, garnishing with 2 teaspoons toasted sesame seeds.

Sautéed Tender Greens with Raisins and Almonds

Follow Master Recipe, making these changes: Increase garlic to 3 cloves. Cook ¼ teaspoon hot red pepper flakes with garlic. Add ⅓ cup golden raisins with wet greens and proceed with recipe. When greens have wilted, add ½ teaspoon minced lemon zest. When greens are done, stir in 3 tablespoons toasted slivered almonds. Serve immediately.

👑

Master Recipe

Quick-Cooked Tough Greens
serves four

➤ **N O T E :** *With the exception of turnip greens, all tough greens can be stemmed using the method outlined in figure 11. See figures 12 and 13, page 61, when working with turnip greens. Shallow-blanched greens should be shocked in cold water to stop the cooking process, drained, and then braised.*

	Salt
2	pounds assertive greens, such as kale, collards, mustard, or turnip greens, stemmed, washed in several changes of cold water, and coarsely chopped
2	large garlic cloves, sliced thin
¼	teaspoon hot red pepper flakes
3	tablespoons extra-virgin olive oil
⅓-½	cup chicken stock or low-sodium canned broth
	Lemon wedges (optional)

⁞ **I N S T R U C T I O N S :**

1. Bring 2 quarts water to boil in soup kettle or other large pot. Add 1½ teaspoons salt and greens and stir until wilted. Cover and cook until greens are just tender, about 7 min-

6 5

utes. Drain in colander. Rinse kettle with cold water to cool, then refill with cold water. Place greens in cold water to stop cooking process. Gather handful of greens, lift out of water, and squeeze until only droplets fall from them. Repeat with remaining greens.

2. Heat garlic, red pepper flakes, and oil in large sauté pan over medium heat until garlic starts to sizzle. Add greens and stir to coat with oil. Add ⅓ cup stock, cover, and cook over medium-high heat, adding more stock if necessary, until greens are tender and juicy and most of stock has been absorbed, about 5 minutes. Adjust seasonings, adding salt and red pepper flakes to taste. Serve immediately.

▓ VARIATIONS:

Quick-Cooked Tough Greens with Prosciutto
Follow Master Recipe and after garlic starts to sizzle, add 1 ounce thin-sliced prosciutto that has been cut into thin strips. Add greens and proceed as directed, stirring in ¼ teaspoon grated lemon zest just before serving.

Quick-Cooked Tough Greens with Red Bell Pepper
Follow Master Recipe, sautéing ½ thinly sliced red bell pepper in oil until softened, about 4 minutes, before adding garlic and red pepper flakes. Proceed as directed.

Quick-Cooked Tough Greens with Black Olives and Lemon Zest

Follow Master Recipe, adding ⅓ cup pitted and chopped black olives, such as kalamatas, after garlic starts to sizzle. Add greens and proceed as directed, stirring in ¼ teaspoon grated lemon zest just before serving.

Quick-Cooked Tough Greens with Bacon and Onion

Fry 2 bacon slices, cut crosswise into thin strips, in large sauté pan over medium heat until crisp, about 5 minutes. Remove bacon with slotted spoon and drain on paper towels. If necessary, add canola oil to bacon drippings to bring up to 2 tablespoons. Follow step 1 of Master Recipe, blanching and draining greens as directed. Cook 1 small onion, minced, and 2 minced garlic cloves (in place of sliced garlic cloves and hot red pepper flakes) in bacon fat/oil mixture until softened, about 4 minutes. Add greens and proceed as directed, sprinkling with bacon bits and 2 teaspoons cider vinegar just before serving.

chapter nine

PEAS

THERE ARE THREE VARIETIES OF PEAS SOLD in most markets—shell peas, sugar snap peas, and snow peas. Shell peas are generally mealy and bland. Frozen peas are usually sweeter and better-tasting, but since fresh sugar snap and snow peas are almost always available, we prefer not to use frozen peas for side dishes.

The flat, light-green snow pea has a long history, especially in the Chinese kitchen. The peas are tiny and the pod is tender enough to eat. Sugar snap peas are a relatively recent development dating back just 20 years. They are a cross between shell peas and snow peas. The sweet, crisp pod is edible and holds small, juicy peas.

Sugar snap and snow peas should be cooked quickly so that they retain some crunch and color. Stir-frying works well with snow peas, which have a fairly sturdy pod. However, sugar snap peas are too delicate for such intense heat. We found the pods will become mushy by the time the peas inside are actually heated through.

Both kinds of peas can be steamed, but we found that they respond better to blanching in salted water. The salt balances some of their sweetness and brings out their flavor. Blanched peas tend to shrivel or pucker as they cool. To solve this problem, we plunge the cooked peas into ice water as soon as they are drained. This also helps to set their bright color. Once cooled, the peas can be drained, patted dry, and briefly sautéed in butter or oil to heat them through and add flavor.

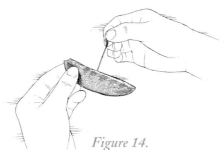

Figure 14.

To prepare snow peas, remove the string that runs along the flat side of the pod before cooking. Rip off the tip of the snow pea and pull along the pod to remove the string at the same time.

♛

Master Recipe

Blanched Sugar Snap Peas
or Snow Peas
serves four

➤ **NOTE:** *Sugar snap and snow peas may be cooked and seasoned the same way. The only difference is the cooking time. Have a bowl of ice water ready to shock the drained peas and prevent further softening and shriveling. The peas should be seasoned and reheated as directed in variations.*

1 teaspoon salt
4 cups loosely packed sugar snap peas or snow peas (about 1 pound), tips pulled off and strings removed from snow peas (*see* figure 14, page 69)

▦ INSTRUCTIONS:

Bring 6 cups water to boil in large saucepan. Add salt and peas and cook until crisp-tender, 1½ to 2 minutes for sugar snap peas or about 2½ minutes for snow peas. Drain peas, shock in ice water, drain again, and pat dry. (Peas can be set aside for 1 hour before seasoning.)

▦ VARIATIONS:

Peas with Hazelnut Butter and Sage
Cook peas as directed in Master Recipe and set aside. Toast 2 tablespoons chopped hazelnuts in small skillet, shaking

70

pan often to promote even cooking, just until fragrant, 3 to 4 minutes. Heat 2 tablespoons unsalted butter in medium sauté pan over medium heat until it browns to color of brown sugar and smells nutty, about 5 minutes. (Take care not to burn.) Add peas, 2 tablespoons chopped fresh sage leaves, and nuts. Toss to combine and cook until peas are heated through, 1 to 1½ minutes. Season with salt and pepper to taste and serve immediately.

Peas with Ham and Mint

Cook peas as directed in Master Recipe and set aside. Melt 1 tablespoon unsalted butter in medium sauté pan over medium heat. Add ½ cup country or smoked ham, cut into ¼-inch dice, and sauté for 1 minute. Add peas and 2 tablespoons chopped fresh mint. Toss to combine and cook until peas are heated through, 1 to 1½ minutes. Season with salt and pepper to taste and serve immediately.

Peas with Lemon, Garlic, and Basil

Cook peas as directed in Master Recipe and set aside. Heat 2 tablespoons extra-virgin olive oil in medium sauté pan over medium heat. Add zest of 1 lemon, sliced very fine, and 1 minced garlic clove, and sauté until garlic is golden, about 2 minutes. Add peas, 1 tablespoon lemon juice, and 8 chopped fresh basil leaves. Toss to combine and cook until peas are heated through, 1 to 1½ minutes. Season with salt and pepper to taste and serve immediately.

Master Recipe

Stir-Fried Snow Peas
serves four

➤ **NOTE:** *Snow peas are sturdier than sugar snap peas and hold up well when stir-fried.*

¼	cup chicken stock or canned low-sodium broth
¼	teaspoon salt
	Ground black pepper
1	tablespoon plus 1 teaspoon peanut oil
4	cups loosely packed snow peas (about 1 pound), tips pulled off and strings removed (*see* figure 14, page 69)
1½	teaspoons minced garlic
1½	teaspoons minced fresh gingerroot

▦ **INSTRUCTIONS:**

1. Mix chicken stock, salt, and pepper to taste in small bowl.

2. Heat 12-inch nonstick skillet over high heat until quite hot, 2 to 3 minutes. Add 1 tablespoon oil and swirl to coat bottom of pan (oil should shimmer immediately). Add snow peas and cook for 2 minutes, tossing peas every 30 seconds.

3. Clear center of pan, add garlic and ginger, and drizzle with remaining 1 teaspoon oil. Mash garlic and ginger with back of spatula. Cook for 10 seconds and then mix with snow peas. Off heat, add chicken stock mixture (it should immediately reduce down to a glaze). Serve at once.

⋮⋮ VARIATIONS:

Stir-Fried Snow Peas with Oyster Sauce
Follow Master Recipe, substituting mixture of 3 tablespoons dry sherry, 2 tablespoons oyster sauce, 1 tablespoon Asian sesame oil, 1 tablespoon soy sauce, and ¼ teaspoon ground black pepper for chicken stock mixture in step 1.

Stir-Fried Snow Peas with Spicy Orange Sauce
Follow Master Recipe, substituting mixture of 3 tablespoons dry sherry, 1 tablespoon soy sauce, 1 tablespoon Asian sesame oil, 2 teaspoons red wine vinegar, ½ teaspoon sugar, ½ teaspoon ground black pepper, and ¼ teaspoon salt for chicken stock mixture in step 1. Add 1 tablespoon grated orange zest and ¼ teaspoon hot red pepper flakes along with garlic and ginger.

chapter ten

≷

PEPPERS

MOST COOKS ARE FAMILIAR WITH ROAST-ing bell peppers for salads or dips. However, peppers may be sliced and cooked as a vegetable side dish as well. Green peppers are unripe and generally quite bitter. Red, yellow, and orange peppers are all fully ripe and much sweeter. Avoid purple peppers, which turn a drab green color when cooked and cost much more than green peppers.

We tested sautéing and stir-frying first and found that both methods yield lightly seared peppers that are still fairly crisp. They were good, but lacked the silky smoothness of roasted peppers. We tried longer cooking times, but the exterior charred by the time the pepper was fully cooked.

We decided to see what would happen if we put the cover on the skillet after searing them. As we hoped, the peppers steamed in their own juices and became especially tender. We found that the moisture from the peppers is enough to keep them from scorching in the covered pan. We also realized that we now had an opportunity to add another liquid for juicier, seasoned peppers. A little vinegar balances the intense sweetness of the peppers and works especially well.

Figure 15.
To prepare peppers, cut around the stem with a small, sharp knife. Pull out the stem and the attached core, which should be filled with seeds.

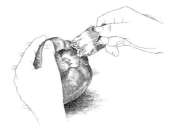

Figure 16.
To easily remove the white ribs and make the pepper flatter for slicing, cut the pepper lengthwise into quarters. Slide a knife under the white ribs to remove them as well as remaining seeds. Slice the cleaned pepper lengthwise into ¼-inch-wide strips.

7 5

♥

Master Recipe

Sautéed Bell Peppers
serves four

➤ NOTE: *A mixture of yellow, orange, and red peppers delivers the sweetest and best results. You may use one green pepper, but these unripe peppers are much less sweet and should not be used in greater amounts.*

2   tablespoons extra-virgin olive oil
4   medium bell peppers (about 1¾ pounds),
    cored, seeded, and cut into ¼-inch-wide strips
    (*see* figures 15 and 16, page 75)
1   medium garlic clove, minced
1   tablespoon chopped fresh oregano, basil, or
    parsley leaves
    Salt and ground black pepper

⁞ INSTRUCTIONS:

1. Heat oil in large skillet over medium-high heat. Add peppers and sauté, tossing occasionally, until peppers begin to brown on edges, about 5 minutes.

2. Add garlic and cook for 1 minute. Reduce heat to low, cover pan, and cook until peppers are tender, 4 to 5 minutes.

Remove cover and stir in herb. Season with salt and pepper to taste. Serve hot, warm, or at room temperature.

⠿ VARIATIONS:

Sautéed Bell Peppers with Red Onion and Balsamic Vinegar

Follow Master Recipe, cooking 1 small red onion, thinly sliced, with bell peppers. Just before covering pan, add 3 tablespoons balsamic vinegar. Use parsley as herb.

Sautéed Bell Peppers with Black Olives and Feta Cheese

Follow Master Recipe, adding 2 tablespoons red wine vinegar to pan just before covering. Use oregano as herb and add 8 pitted and chopped black olives at the same time. Just before serving, crumble 2 ounces feta cheese over peppers.

Sautéed Bell Peppers with Bacon and Caraway

Fry 4 bacon slices, cut crosswise into ¼-inch-wide strips, in large skillet over medium heat until crisp, about 5 minutes. Remove bacon from pan with slotted spoon and drain on paper towels. Proceed with Master Recipe, using bacon drippings instead of olive oil and adding 1 medium chopped onion to drippings with peppers. Omit garlic. Just before covering pan, add 2 tablespoons cider vinegar and 1 teaspoon caraway seeds. Replace herb with bacon. Serve hot.

chapter eleven

TOMATOES

TOMATOES ARE A STAPLE IN SUMMER SAL-
ads. The mildly acidic juices from the
tomatoes themselves provide a proper
base for a dressing with little or no additional vinegar or other acid. To make this work, you need
to extract a little of the juice from the tomatoes before you
make salads. Simply cut the tomatoes into wedges, sprinkle them with salt, and wait about 15 minutes for the juices
to exude.

To serve round (or beefsteak) tomatoes as a side dish, it's
best to combine them with bread crumbs and bake them.
There are two choices—the tomatoes may be cored and

stuffed, or they may be halved and sprinkled with the crumbs. We tested both methods and found that all the liquid material in the tomatoes must be removed to get the crumbs to brown and crisp in the oven. This is easier to do when the tomatoes are halved and sprinkled with crumbs. It's hard to remove all the seeds from a whole cored tomato. It's also tricky to get much stuffing into a whole cored tomato, while a halved tomato has plenty of moist surface area to which crumbs can adhere.

We found it best to bake the tomatoes as quickly as possible—you want the crumbs to brown but don't want the tomatoes to soften too much. An oven temperature of 400 degrees delivered the best results in our testing, quickly crisping the crumbs and allowing the tomatoes to warm through and soften slightly but still hold their shape.

For a quicker side dish, try sautéing cherry tomatoes. The idea is to get them in and out of the pan quickly, so they don't become mushy and fall apart. We found that medium-high heat does the best job. In our testing, we found that many cherry tomatoes are slightly bitter. We liked the results when we sprinkled a little sugar over the tomatoes before they went into the pan. If your cherry tomatoes are especially sweet, you may omit the sugar, but in most cases we find that it helps balances the acidity in the tomatoes.

♛

Master Recipe

Tomato Salad with Olives and Capers

serves four

➤ **NOTE:** *Salting the tomato wedges creates the juices that form the base of the dressing for the salad.*

4-5	large vine-ripened tomatoes (about 1½ pounds)
½	teaspoon salt
3	tablespoons extra-virgin olive oil
1	tablespoon lemon juice
3	tablespoons capers, chopped
12	large black olives, such as kalamatas, pitted and chopped
¼	cup finely chopped red onion
2	tablespoons chopped fresh parsley leaves Ground black pepper

▓ INSTRUCTIONS:

1. Core and halve tomatoes through stem end, then cut each half into 4 or 5 wedges. Toss wedges and salt in large bowl; let rest until small pool of liquid accumulates, 15 to 20 minutes.

2. Meanwhile, whisk oil, lemon juice, capers, olives, onion, parsley, and pepper to taste in small bowl. Pour mixture over tomatoes and accumulated juices and toss to coat. Set aside to blend flavors, about 5 minutes. Serve.

:: VARIATIONS:

Tomato and Bread Salad with Garlic-Anchovy Dressing

Follow step 1 of Master Recipe. Whisk together 3 tablespoons extra-virgin olive oil, 1½ tablespoons red wine vinegar, 2 minced garlic cloves, ⅓ cup chopped fresh basil leaves, 3 minced anchovy fillets, and ground black pepper to taste in small bowl. Toss dressing with tomatoes and set aside for 5 minutes. Add 4 slices of chewy country-style bread, cut ¾ inch thick, that have been toasted or grilled until lightly browned and then cut into ¾-inch cubes. Serve immediately.

Tomato and Cucumber Salad

Peel, quarter, seed, and cut 2 cucumbers into ¼-inch dice. Toss with 2 teaspoons salt in strainer set over bowl, and set aside for 1 hour; discard liquid. Follow Step 1 of Master Recipe. Whisk together 3 tablespoons extra-virgin olive oil, 2 tablespoons lemon juice, ¼ cup finely chopped red onion, ¼ cup chopped fresh mint leaves, and ground black pepper to taste. Toss tomatoes in dressing and set aside for 5 minutes. Add drained cucumbers and serve immediately.

Master Recipe

Baked Tomatoes
serves four

➤ **NOTE:** *The key to this recipe is removing the seeds and surrounding gelatinous material. Otherwise, the tomatoes will become soupy and the bread crumb topping will not brown.*

½	cup dried plain bread crumbs
¼	cup grated Parmesan cheese
2	tablespoons chopped fresh basil leaves
2	tablespoons chopped fresh oregano leaves
2	medium garlic cloves, minced
¼	teaspoon hot red pepper flakes
3	tablespoons extra-virgin olive oil
4	medium ripe tomatoes (about 1¼ pounds), halved and seeded (*see* figure 17)
	Salt and ground black pepper

INSTRUCTIONS:

1. Preheat oven to 400 degrees. Mix crumbs, cheese, basil, oregano, garlic, hot red pepper flakes, and 1 tablespoon oil together in small bowl. Set aside.

2. Place tomato halves, cut side up, in single layer in 13 by 9-inch baking dish. Season tomatoes with salt and pepper to taste. Spoon bread crumb mixture evenly over tomato halves. Drizzle remaining 2 tablespoons oil over bread crumbs.

3. Bake until tomatoes are cooked through and bread crumbs are crisp and golden brown, 25 to 30 minutes. Remove dish from oven and let cool for 5 to 10 minutes. Serve warm.

▪▪ **VARIATION:**

Baked Tomatoes with Olives and Balsamic Vinegar
Follow Master Recipe, adding 8 pitted and chopped black olives to bread crumb mixture. Just before serving, drizzle tomatoes with 1½ tablespoons balsamic vinegar.

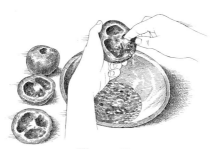

Figure 17.
To prepare round tomatoes for baking, remove the core and then cut the tomatoes in half around the equator. Use your finger to pull out the seeds and surrounding gelatinous material from each tomato half.

♛

Master Recipe

Sautéed Cherry Tomatoes
serves four

➤ **NOTE:** *To speed up the caramelization process and balance the acidity of the tomatoes, we tossed the cherry tomatoes with a little sugar just before cooking. If your cherry tomatoes are very sweet, you may want to reduce or omit the sugar.*

1   tablespoon extra-virgin olive oil
4   cups (2 pints) red cherry tomatoes, halved unless very small
2   teaspoons sugar
1   medium garlic clove, minced
2   tablespoons thinly sliced fresh basil leaves
     Salt and ground black pepper

INSTRUCTIONS:

1. Heat oil in large skillet over medium-high heat until shimmering.

2. Mix tomatoes and sugar in medium bowl and add to hot oil. (Do not mix tomatoes ahead of time or you will draw off some juices.) Cook 1 minute, tossing frequently. Add garlic and mix, cooking another 30 seconds. Remove pan from heat, add basil, and season with salt and pepper to taste. Serve immediately.

⁝ VARIATIONS:

Sautéed Cherry Tomatoes with Curry and Mint

Follow Master Recipe, adding 1½ teaspoons curry powder with garlic. Substitute thinly sliced mint leaves for basil. If you like, mix in 2 tablespoons plain yogurt just before serving.

Sautéed Cherry Tomatoes with Brown Butter and Herbs

Follow Master Recipe, replacing oil with equal amount of unsalted butter. When butter starts to brown and foam subsides, add tomatoes and sugar and cook as directed. Substitute equal amount of snipped chives or minced fresh dill or tarragon for basil.

chapter twelve

ZUCCHINI & SUMMER SQUASH

THE BIGGEST PROBLEM THAT CONFRONTS the cook when preparing zucchini and yellow summer squash is their wateriness. Both are about 95 percent water and will become soupy if just thrown into a hot pan. If they cook in their own juices, they won't brown. Since both are fairly bland, they really benefit from some browning. Clearly, some of the water must be removed before sautéing.

We tested salting to draw off some water and found that sliced and salted zucchini will shed about 20 percent of its weight after sitting for 30 minutes. (Summer squash performed the same in all of our tests.) One pound of sliced zucchini threw off almost three tablespoons of liquid, further confirmation that salting works. We tested longer periods and found that little moisture is extracted after 30 minutes.

Given that you don't always have 30 minutes, we wanted to develop quicker methods for cooking zucchini. We tried shredding the zucchini on the large holes of a box grater and then squeezing out excess water by hand. We were able to reduce the weight of shredded zucchini by 25 percent by wrapping it in paper towels and squeezing until dry. Shredded and squeezed zucchini cooked up nicely, although it did not brown as well as sliced and salted zucchini.

After our success with shredding and squeezing, we wondered if a similar technique might work with sliced zucchini. Since sliced zucchini has so much less surface area than shredded zucchini, we found our manual method of extracting water to be ineffective; we recommend salting in this case.

Another quick-prep option is the grill. The intense heat quickly expels excess moisture in zucchini, and that moisture harmlessly drops down on the coals rather than sitting in the pan. We found that so much evaporation occurs during grilling that salting or shredding is not necessary.

Master Recipe

Shredded Zucchini or Summer Squash Sauté
serves four

➤ **N O T E :** *Try this recipe when you're pressed for time and want to cook indoors.*

3   tablespoons extra-virgin olive oil
5   medium zucchini or summer squash
    (about 2 pounds), trimmed, shredded, and
    squeezed dry (*see* figures 18 and 19)
3   medium garlic cloves, minced
2   tablespoons minced fresh parsley, basil, mint,
    tarragon, or chives
    Salt and ground black pepper

I N S T R U C T I O N S :

Heat oil in large nonstick skillet over medium-high heat. Add zucchini or squash and garlic and cook, stirring occasionally, until tender, about 7 minutes. Stir in herb and salt and pepper to taste. Serve immediately.

V A R I A T I O N S :

Shredded Zucchini or Summer Squash and Carrot Sauté
Follow Master Recipe, substituting 2 medium peeled and

88

shredded carrots for 1 zucchini or squash.

Creamed Zucchini or Summer Squash

Follow Master Recipe, substituting an equal amount of butter for oil. Omit garlic and add ⅓ cup heavy cream with herb; simmer briefly until cream is absorbed.

Figure 18.
For quick indoor cooking, shred trimmed zucchini or squash on the large holes of a box grater or in a food processor fitted with the shredding disk.

Figure 19.
Wrap the shredded zucchini or squash in paper towels and squeeze out excess liquid. Proceed immediately with sautéing.

89

Master Recipe

Grilled Zucchini or Summer Squash
serves four

➤ NOTE: *Excess water evaporates over hot coals so no salting of zucchini or squash is necessary before cooking.*

4   medium zucchini or summer squash
     (about 1½ pounds), trimmed and sliced
     lengthwise into ½-inch-thick strips
2   tablespoons extra-virgin olive oil
     Salt and ground black pepper

INSTRUCTIONS:

1. Light grill. Lay zucchini or squash on large baking sheet and brush both sides with oil. Sprinkle generously with salt and pepper.

2. Place zucchini or squash on grill. Cook, turning once, until marked with dark strips, 8 to 10 minutes. Remove from grill and serve hot, warm, or at room temperature.

■■ VARIATIONS:

Grilled Zucchini or Summer Squash with Tomatoes and Basil

Whisk 2 tablespoons extra-virgin olive oil with 1 tablespoon balsamic vinegar and salt and pepper to taste in large serving bowl. Add 2 tablespoons minced fresh basil leaves and 1 large tomato, cored and cut into thin wedges, and toss. Follow Master Recipe, cutting grilled zucchini or squash into 1-inch pieces when cooled slightly. Toss zucchini or squash with tomatoes and serve warm or at room temperature.

Grilled Zucchini or Summer Squash with Capers and Oregano

Whisk 1 tablespoon chopped capers, 1 tablespoon red wine vinegar, and 1 medium minced garlic clove in small bowl. Whisk in 2 tablespoons extra-virgin olive oil and season with salt and pepper to taste. Follow Master Recipe, cutting grilled zucchini or squash into 1-inch pieces when cooled slightly. Toss zucchini or squash with dressing and 1 table-spoon chopped fresh oregano in large bowl. Serve warm or at room temperature.

👑

Master Recipe

Sautéed Zucchini or Summer Squash

serves four

➢ **NOTE**: *If you like browned zucchini or squash, you must salt it before cooking. Salting drives off excess water and helps the zucchini or squash sauté rather than stew in its own juices. Coarse kosher salt does the best job of driving off liquid and can be wiped away without rinsing. Do not add more salt when cooking or the dish will be too salty.*

4	medium zucchini or summer squash (about 1½ pounds), trimmed and sliced crosswise into ¼-inch rounds
1	tablespoon kosher salt
3	tablespoons extra-virgin olive oil
1	small onion or 2 large shallots, minced
1	teaspoon grated lemon zest
1	tablespoon lemon juice
1-2	tablespoons minced fresh parsley, basil, mint, tarragon, or chives
	Ground black pepper

▦ **INSTRUCTIONS**:

1. Place zucchini or squash slices in colander and sprinkle

92

with salt. Set colander over bowl until about ⅓ cup water drains from zucchini or squash, about 30 minutes. Remove vegetable from colander and pat dry with clean kitchen towel or several paper towels, wiping off any remaining crystals of salt.

2. Heat oil in large skillet over medium heat. Add onion or shallots and sauté until almost softened, about 2 minutes. Increase heat to medium-high and add zucchini or squash and lemon zest. Sauté until zucchini or squash is golden brown, about 10 minutes. Stir in lemon juice and herb and season with pepper to taste. Serve immediately.

▪▪ **VARIATIONS:**

Sautéed Zucchini or Summer Squash with Walnuts and Herbs

Follow Master Recipe, omitting lemon zest and juice and adding 2 tablespoons toasted chopped walnuts with herb.

Sautéed Zucchini or Summer Squash with Olives and Lemon

Follow Master Recipe, adding ¼ cup pitted and chopped black olives along with lemon juice and using 2 teaspoons minced fresh thyme or oregano as herb.

Sautéed Zucchini or Summer Squash with Pancetta and Parsley

Follow Master Recipe, omitting oil. After salting zucchini or squash, cook 2 ounces diced pancetta or bacon in skillet. When fat renders, add onion and continue with recipe. Omit lemon zest and juice and use parsley as herb.

index

9 5